When We Have
Failed —What Next?

*"A bruised reed he will not break,
and a smoldering wick he will not snuff
out, till he leads justice to victory."*

Matthew 12:20

When We Have Failed —What Next?

God's Answer

to Our Failures

K.P. Yohannan

BOOKS

a division of Gospel for Asia

www.gfa.org

When We Have Failed—What Next?

© 2006 by K.P. Yohannan

All rights reserved.

ISBN 978-1-59589-035-1

Published by gfa books, a division of Gospel for Asia
1800 Golden Trail Court, Carrollton TX 75010 USA
phone: (972) 300-7777
fax: (972) 300-7778

Printed in the United States of America

For information about other materials, visit our website: www.gfa.org.

Table of Contents

Introduction

I once heard about a man whose memory was failing. He went to his doctor to seek treatment. After this man had gone through various tests, his doctor's conclusion was, "I want to be of help, but in my opinion, we only have one option. I can do surgery to prevent you from losing more of your memory, but you need to know that in the process you could lose your eyesight."

The doctor then left his patient with time to decide whether or not he wanted to go through with the treatment. On the doctor's return, the man seeking help responded, "I've thought about it and decided not to have the surgery. I'd rather have my eyesight than my memory. I prefer to see where I'm going rather than remember where I've been."

Although this is obviously not a true story, how many of us desperately wish we *could* in their entirety forget the failures of our past? So many of us don't experience joy in its fullest because we are still tethered to the sins of yesterday.

We cannot change the past no matter how wishful we may be. We can, however, learn from it. That's certainly better than being held captive to its regrets, setbacks and problems.

Every morning you awake to a new gift— the gift of *today*. It is my prayer that through this booklet you will be freed to let go of yesterday—learn from it, yes, but also let go of it—and then to embrace today. For today *is* full of hope.

" 'For I know the plans I have for you,' declares the LORD, 'plans to prosper you and not to harm you, plans to give you hope and a future' " (Jeremiah 29:11).

I believe this small booklet is one of God's ways of extending hope to you right now. Please reach out and receive its truth. May God bless you.

CHAPTER ONE

There Is Hope

Robert Robinson lived in the 18th century. Converted through George Whitefield's preaching, he himself went on to become the Methodist minister who wrote the famous hymn "Come, Thou Fount of Every Blessing." You probably remember the lines:

> *Come, Thou Fount of every blessing,*
> *Tune my heart to sing Thy grace;*
> *Streams of mercy, never ceasing,*
> *Call for songs of loudest praise.*[1]

In his latter years, Robinson wandered from the faith to pursue the pleasures of this world. While riding on a stagecoach during this time, he sat by a woman deeply fascinated by a book she was reading. When she came across a lyric she considered especially beautiful, she turned to Robinson and said, "I am reading something wonderful. What do you think about it?" This is what she read:

> Prone to wander, Lord, I feel it,
> Prone to leave the God I love.[2]

She had no idea she was sitting next to the very man who had penned those words years earlier.

Upon remembering the song and the man he once was, Robinson broke down. With tears he replied, "Madam, I am the poor, unhappy man who composed that hymn many years ago. I would give a thousand worlds, if I had them, to enjoy the feelings I had then." Through this encounter, Robinson was brought back into the outstretched arms of his loving God.

This story of restoration at the end of sin's winding road is neither the first, nor will it be the last. From the beginning of time, history has demonstrated that there is hope for the one who has fallen.

The fact that you picked up this booklet shows that you too are seeking for that reassuring hope. I want you to know there *is* hope. Our failures are no surprise to God. He knows, with greater understanding than we, the creation He made. And this One, who sees our sins, also knows His purposes for us.

History Reveals

In the Bible, God left us the complete stories of spiritual giants through whom He worked—Moses, Elijah, David and many more—just as they were, flaws and all. He did not touch up the negatives or use Photoshop to present them in a better light. There was no cover-up.

Look at Moses. What an incredible life story is his—forsaken at birth and then rescued by Pharaoh's daughter. He was raised in a powerful family of influence. As an adult, Moses' heart was burdened for his people, and he spoke out against the cruel slavery inflicted upon the children of Israel. Unfortunately, he "ruined" what he felt God had called him to do by killing a man and subsequently spent 40 years hiding in the desert.

Remember that Moses was a real human being with the same feelings as you and I. Forty years is a long time to contemplate failure. When the Lord eventually came to offer him hope and unfold His rescue plan, Moses responded that God was making a mistake and that He should look for someone else (see Exodus 4:10, 13).

Elijah—the great prophet of God—was one who, in a time of terrible discouragement, simply said, "I want to die" (see 1 Kings 19:4). Talk about singing the blues!

David is another classic example. This shepherd boy turned king seemed to take the worst fall of them all. This national hero who began so well, anointed by God and considered a man after His own heart, fell into adultery and then murdered the woman's husband to cover it up (see 2 Samuel 11). Does it get much worse than that?

Why does God show us the failures of these great leaders? Could it be He wants us to know that in spite of our fiascoes, He can still make something glorious out of our lives?

The list of names in Hebrews 11 underscores this truth. In this passage, men and women of great faith are noted—ones whom God Almighty approved. One might be shocked, however, to discover how many of them were restored spiritually following failures such as deception, drunkenness, adultery, idolatry and murder.

Consider Jacob. What a saga his life story is. From birth, God gave him a remarkable promise that he would be blessed and his older brother would serve him. With this kind of divine assurance, it would seem like Jacob would turn out to be the perfect saint. Instead, he became a crook who lied to his own father, stole his blessing and lived a life full of deceit. Jacob ended up wasting 20 precious years of his life.

I consider his biography one of the most interesting of them all. Here is why: Numerous times throughout the Bible, God reminds His people that He is "the God of Abraham, the God of Isaac and the God of Jacob" (Exodus 3:15). In fact, in this same verse, God says, "This is my name forever, the name by which I am to be remembered from generation to generation."

Toward the end of Jacob's journey, God changed his name, which means "deceiver," to Israel, meaning "Prince of God." So, why doesn't He say, "I am the God of Abraham, Isaac and . . . *Israel*"? How strange! How come He associates His name with a cheat who wasted two decades trying to do things his own way?

Through His name, His very identity, God wants to say to you and me, "I am still the God who makes failures into princes of God. I remain the God who takes broken lives— people with multiple divorces, sick in body because of sin, in prison for decades, labeled as losers, crazy folk nobody wants, outcasts with no hope—and turns them into some- thing beautiful."

Beauty for Ashes

The nation of Israel was betrothed to God. Yet she cast her beauty before every possible lover she could find, forsaking her true suitor. As we read through Psalm 78, we see time and again God's faithfulness displayed in contrast to Israel's unfaithfulness. In spite of her vulgar idolatry and the terrible offering of human sacrifices, God did not cut Israel off forever.

What does God say about her? " 'You have played the harlot with many lovers; Yet return to Me,' says the LORD" (Jeremiah 3:1, NKJV). Instead of deserting Israel because of her countless sins, He declares that there is hope, saying, "I will win her back once again. I will lead her out into the desert and speak tenderly to her there. I will return her vineyards to her and transform the Valley of Trouble into a gateway of hope" (Hosea 2:14–15, NLT). These are gracious words from the living God about His adulterous people.

Today there is a gateway of hope. God is the original and ultimate rescuer. And for all who want to be rescued, He is able.

> *There is no sin too great,*
> *God cannot forgive it.*
> *There is no loss,*
> *He cannot restore.*
> *There is no scar,*
> *He cannot heal.*

> *There is no distance you can go,*
> *His grace cannot reach.*
> *There is nothing—absolutely nothing—*
> *to stop His love and mercy for you.*
> *If there is breath in your being,*
> *there is hope.*
> *There is hope.*[3]

The thief on the cross confessed that he failed miserably and admitted he deserved the horrible death he was dying. It was all over for him—hell waited, its mouth open to devour him. At least that was what he believed. Yet because of his confession and the marvelous grace of God, he made it into paradise that very day with the Son of God (see Luke 23:43).

It is never too late. God is not mad at you. He is, in fact, for you. Don't give up. Mighty to save and faithful to love is He (see Zephaniah 3:17–19). It is to the very ones who know the pain of personal failure that He comes and extends hope:

> He has sent me to bind up the broken-hearted, . . . to comfort all who mourn, . . . to bestow on them a crown of *beauty instead of ashes,* the oil of *gladness instead of mourning,* and a garment of *praise instead of a spirit of despair.* They *will be called oaks of righteousness,* a planting of the LORD for the display of his splendor (Isaiah 61:1–3, emphasis mine).

Maybe you are like Robert Robinson who wandered away from the God he once loved. Perhaps you revisited a sin from the past you thought you were through with. You may be living with painful memories of what once was or simply shaking your head at a sin that seems to surface too regularly.

In any case, whatever letdown you are facing, whether considerable or minor, my sincere prayer is that in Robinson's words, you will experience God's "streams of mercy, never ceasing." Another line from this same hymn I have been quoting reads:

> *And I hope, by Thy good pleasure,*
> *Safely to arrive at home.*[4]

Is that your hope? Then let today mark a new beginning for you.

CHAPTER TWO

I Can't Believe I Did That!

Growing up in a respectable family in his community, Roy led a life of affluence with a bright future before him. His father, a successful medical doctor, was so proud when his son decided to enter medical college.

Then right before his eyes, all that looked so promising began to collapse like a deck of cards. A new school brought him new friends. But these colleagues were living on the edge, and their company took Roy on a downward spiral.

After only two years in medical college, nothing seemed to be going right. He was into drugs, and with his new pastime, his health began to waste away and his grades were slipping—he was failing. To top it off, this wayward student found out he was going to be fathering a child. His world *was* falling apart around him.

His parents got wind of his wild life and were completely devastated. Roy found himself shaking his head saying, "I just can't believe how it all happened." In essence, he was saying, "I can't believe I did this!" Then when things could not get much worse, Roy's best friend, who had always been there no matter what, jumped off a 12-story building and committed suicide.

Can it get any worse? I believe there is a key New Testament personality who would answer, "Yes, it can!" Maybe we should look briefly at a mortifying part of his story as told in all four of the Gospels.

> Then seizing him [Jesus], they led him away and took him into the house of the high priest. Peter followed at a distance. But when they had kindled a fire in the middle of the courtyard and had sat down together, Peter sat down with them. A servant girl saw him seated there in the firelight. She looked closely at him and said, "This man was with him."
>
> But he denied it. "Woman, I don't know him," he said.
>
> A little later someone else saw him and said, "You also are one of them."
>
> "Man, I am not!" Peter replied.

About an hour later another asserted, "Certainly this fellow was with him, for he is a Galilean."

Peter replied, "Man, I don't know what you're talking about!" Just as he was speaking, the rooster crowed. *The Lord turned and looked straight at Peter* (Luke 22:54–61, emphasis mine).

What a horrific moment that must have been. The Son of God had heard Peter's hot words of denial, and after listening, Jesus, the prisoner, turned and looked straight at His disciple.

What a dreadful turn of events for Peter. In his wildest dreams, he never would have believed himself capable of what he had just done. We know this was traumatic for him, because the passage reports that "he went outside and wept bitterly" (Luke 22:62).

I Can't Believe I Did That!

Chances are you can recall a time in your own life when you "wept bitterly" over something. Like Peter, what you thought could never happen to you did indeed, leaving you ashamed . . .

confused . . .

uncomfortable . . .

frightened . . .

conscience-stricken.

Maybe it was a divorce that threw off your normal equilibrium or a marriage that underwent severe stress. Perhaps it was a business failure that made your life so wretched or an important relationship in which miscommunication and hurt feelings took over. Could it have been the belief that you failed someone important, even yourself? You fell so far short of your personal expectations. Whatever it was, you couldn't believe this was happening, not to you anyway.

Certainly Peter's earlier words, "Lord, I am ready to go with you to prison and to death" (Luke 22:33), came back to mock him. Each of us starts out in life with desires, ambitions and dreams, plus the early commitment and resolve to achieve them. But somewhere along the way, whether by our own deliberate choice or by external circumstances, these aspirations come crashing down before us, crumbling in our hands.

There we sit in the ruins, replaying the various destructive scenes and moaning at the appropriate times, "If only that didn't happen!" Regret clings to our every thought as we struggle to stand with knees made weak by our own choices.

That's where Peter was stuck in his thoughts. Earlier he had so triumphantly announced that Jesus was the Son of the living God. Yes, he was one of those in the "inner circle" closest to his Lord. He even miraculously walked on water. And it was to him that Christ talked about that rock upon which His Church would be built.

But he had just denied the very One he earlier declared to be the Messiah, the man he had said he would follow to the very end and even die for. So much for all his big talk. Jesus had heard with His own ears Peter's strong statements of denial. How could this happen ... *to Peter?*

How Could This Happen?

We all have had those feelings. We think, "How could I have done that? I know better than this. I should have learned by now." Deep inside we have the defense that we are better than the wrong we committed.

Even the worst criminal has all kinds of reasons and explanations for the mess in which he finds himself. For example, "Two Gun" Crowley, responsible for murdering many people in the 1930s, was cornered within a building awaiting an inevitable arrest. He wrote a note while the police were firing at him. The note read, "Under my coat is a weary heart, but a kind one." Then as he faced capital punishment, he questioned his sentence, saying: "This is what I get for defending myself."[1]

In spite of rationalizing and trying to minimize our failure, guilt gnaws at our heart. We sink as we consider what we have done. Yet as followers of God, we know that upon repentance we can experience firsthand His marvelous mercy. Why then do we feel this shadow over us?

Roy Hession puts it so clearly in his book *"When I Saw Him":*

> If you are still mourning and blaming yourself it is not because God is blaming you; He has put the blame on Jesus. It can only be due to one of two things. Either that you have not really repented, or, more likely, you are mourning over your lost righteousness. Perhaps you feel that, having been saved for so long, you should not be failing as you are. . . . You are in effect saying, "Alas for my lost righteousness." That is nothing but pride.[2]

Jesus has taken our blame, the charge against us, the sting of our failure. Then why are we so sick about our failure? Because we *thought* we were better. We regret that our "report card" does not show all the "good marks" we want others to see.

But all the best marks of our own righteousness can only amount to "filthy rags" as the prophet Isaiah says in Isaiah 64:6. They will never be anything we want to showcase.

The only righteousness worthy of displaying is the righteousness of Jesus that we have through His powerful and precious blood.

If what we hang on to is filthy rags, why grasp for it anymore? Why mourn over the loss of it? Will we be like the criminal who until the very end esteemed and held on to "his own righteousness," although obviously it was nothing to boast in?

Paul sums it up in the book of Philippians:

> I consider everything a loss compared to the surpassing greatness of knowing Christ Jesus my Lord, for whose sake I have lost all things. I consider them rubbish, that I may gain Christ and be found in him, not having a righteousness of my own that comes from the law, but that which is through faith in Christ—the righteousness that comes from God and is by faith (3:8–9).

Let us leave our rags behind and hold on to His riches.

He Wept Bitterly

Back to Peter—little wonder this giant of a man ran, brushing aside any outstretched arms that would stop him, to a place outside where he could openly sob his heart out. Crying can be therapeutic. The genuine tears of a naughty child usually quickly touch the heart of a loving parent.

When we are truly saddened by what we have done to hurt the heart of our Savior, those tears of remorse can lead us to repentance. Being vulnerable through them can help bring us to the place of looking Christ in the eye, knowing He saw and heard everything, and telling Him how sorry we are.

Too bad Judas didn't understand this truth. Scripture reports that he was "seized with remorse" (Matthew 27:3). Unfortunately, instead of going to his heavenly Father, he "went away and hanged himself" (Matthew 27:5).

If you have never asked Jesus to be Lord of your life, He is waiting for you with open arms. He has long awaited the time to forgive you of all that you have ever done and draw you into His embrace.

He sees your heartache. He wants to wipe away your tears and give you a fresh start. Don't harden your heart like Judas and walk away.

Simply believe that Jesus is the Son of God, who never sinned, who died for the consequence of your sins and rose to bring you life eternal. Ask Jesus to forgive you of your sins; then commit your life and all that you have into His care and direction.

Your Final Chapters

Remember Roy? That was not the end of his story. After his friend's death, he too considered suicide. But that same week he miraculously heard a Christian radio broadcast. He listened to God's Word, and he too found restoration in Jesus Christ. His life completely changed. His sins and wild life were forgiven. What looked like a life that was lost, became a beacon of light to many.

He married the young lady who was pregnant with his child and finished his schooling. Then he went to one of the hardest regions of North India as a doctor ministering to the poor, bringing his skills and the message of Jesus Christ. Many people have found hope through Roy's life.

For Peter, at that moment when his eyes met the eyes of Jesus, he did not know the end of his own story. He could not comprehend the incredible manner in which Jesus would rise from the dead. He didn't foresee his own restoration taking place on a beach in Galilee a few weeks later. He wasn't yet able to envision the miraculous growth of the New Testament Church and the strategic role he would play in that narrative. All he knew at that instant was how he was spiritually washed out.

Maybe all you see right now is your own failure. But as you ask for God's forgiveness, He sees His perfect righteousness when He looks at you. He sees the beautiful end of your story—it isn't over yet. Those final chapters have yet to be written. The Lord is saying to you, "Your story isn't anywhere near finished!"

Countless times our sovereign and gracious God has heard the bitter cries of His people after they have sinned in ways they never imagined possible. Countless times the Master Potter has shown His great skill as He remolds these vessels into expressions of His glory.

Do you believe that the One who did this for Peter 2,000 years ago can still do the same for you today? He who did it then still does it today. What He did for others, He will do for you.

Take that step: Believe Him.

CHAPTER THREE

No Second Best

Growing up in the southernmost part of India, my friend and I would often pass the potter's house on our way home from school. Stopping to rest under the tall coconut tree in front of his shop, we would watch intently as he and his wife made their clay pots.

Numerous times I stood there mesmerized as he took a lump of clay and began spinning it on his wheel. Soon that which was formless turned almost magically into a beautiful and usable vessel.

Quite often I would observe that what he was working on became marred. Yet the potter was never as disappointed as we were. He knew his craft well. He simply took the piece off the wheel, kneaded the clay again and started over.

This next time it seemed to me the new creation surpassed the one previously attempted.

In Jeremiah 18, the Lord had His prophet watch a potter go through this exact same routine. Then God spoke through His servant, saying, "Like clay in the hand of the potter, so are you in my hand, O house of Israel" (Jeremiah 18:6). These words were intended as both a warning and a message of hope that in spite of repeatedly messing up, God could still make something beautiful of this nation.

All of us have been on God's wheel only to be taken off and repeatedly remolded. Who can't identify with these lines?

> *When God wants to drill a man,*
> *And thrill a man,*
> *And skill a man,*
> *When God wants to mold a man*
> *To play the noblest part;*
> *When He yearns with all His heart*
> *To create so great and bold a man*
> *That all the world will be amazed,*
> *Watch His methods, watch His ways!*
> *How He ruthlessly perfects*
> *Whom He royally elects!*
> *How He hammers him and hurts him,*
> *And with mighty blows converts him*
> *Into trial shapes of clay which*
> *Only God understands;*
> *While his tortured heart is crying,*
> *And he lifts beseeching hands!*

How He bends but never breaks
When his good He undertakes;
How He uses whom He chooses,
And with every purpose fuses him;
By every act induces him
To try His splendor out—
God knows what He's about.[1]

Too often, however, we fight the potter, sometimes sinning grievously in the process. More often than we care to admit, our flaws have been exposed in the protracted process of becoming what God has in mind.

We find ourselves thinking thoughts like, "How do I keep going when I know I am justly reaping what I sowed? What happens if I become physically sick because of my sin (see Psalm 32:3–5)? I can't ask God to heal me because I know this was a road I rebelliously chose to walk down. When it's bankruptcy time, when I crash and burn, what am I left with?"

Unfortunately, our thoughts then lead to, "I've ruined my life. Things can never be the same. I'll never be what God wanted, not with how I messed up this time!" These are the ruminations of being consigned to "second best."

Probably the same thoughts and desperate emotions marked Adam and Eve after hearing the words, "You must leave the Garden," knowing that Paradise was lost at their hands . . . the same for Samson when he was captured and blinded by the Philistines . . .

the same for John Mark when he was kicked off the missionary team.

This is precisely when the devil implements one of his most devious strategies. The enemy isn't really as concerned about our sin as he is our response to it. His intent is that through our collapse, we will simply give up. So he seeks to discourage us to the point at which we lose all hope and even the desire to try anymore.

As I look back on past experiences when I know I failed, it seems the devil always showed up promptly, trying to make my mess-ups seem worse in my mind than they already were. "You're a hopeless case," he would whisper, attempting to drown me in discouragement. You see, he's "the accuser of our brethren, who accused them before our God day and night . . ." (Revelation 12:10, NKJV).

Many times when I've failed, I've felt like I should just toss in the towel. Resign. I've also felt like the worst husband or the most unfit father. Secretly, I wished someone else would just assume my responsibilities, because I certainly didn't believe I was doing a good-enough job.

In such moments when we most need hope, Satan slithers by hissing that hope is all but gone: "There will never be any more hope. Not after what you did!"

But remember that this hellion is a notorious liar. Jesus called him "the father of lies" (John 8:44).

If we foolishly believe the devil's falsifications, we certainly will give up. But if we resist him and lift up our eyes to where our help comes from, we will experience the life-giving restoration that can only come from God. I believe that is why Paul encourages us in 2 Corinthians 4:18 to "fix our eyes not on what is seen [the natural], but on what is unseen [the supernatural]. For what is seen is temporary, but what is unseen is eternal."

God's desire is that through our failure we will allow Him to make us into useful vessels that far surpass the beauty we had before. But this doesn't mean we have to see ourselves as accepting God's second best for our lives. Our failures don't warrant us to live by Plan B rather than the first choice of Plan A. That's not how He thinks.

It's true that sin has its price to pay. But that doesn't prohibit the Lord from doing what He wants through the lives of His children. God remains forever able to fulfill His perfect plan for us. Remember, I said *perfect* plan, the *best* plan, not the second best.

God sees the end from the beginning and knows all things before we even enter the scene. His perfect plan remains.

Was it the devil who introduced that reduced-to-second-best concept? I know this may be hard for some people to believe right now, but I write the truth—God is in the business of making miserable failures into beautiful demonstrations of His mercy and grace.

His ways are above ours. Far above! His original purposes for us are not lost.

The next time it seems the locust and cankerworm have eaten the fruitful life you once knew, look up (see Joel 1:4, KJV). Even if you doubt who you are and how you acted, please don't doubt who He is and how He acts!

When you wake up to the scattered remains of your once-beautiful world looking for strength to carry on, know that this is not the end.

When unexpected storms of severe criticism, slander or even being blacklisted bruise the reed—I tell you the truth, hope still remains.

The next time you fail and wonder whether God is still able to make something—something even better than before—out of your life, you need to know that the answer is 1,000 times, YES! Confident in His skills, God is still totally capable of making everything better.

Never doubt the ability of the divine Master Potter to beautifully refashion flawed pieces. He's been doing it since the beginning of time.

CHAPTER FOUR

Generations Remade

I t began with Creation.
Because God is good and everything He does is good, we can safely assume that all He creates is good. So in the beginning when God created heaven and earth, they were good.

Then something went wrong.

Between Genesis 1:1, when out of His goodness God created the heavens and the earth, and Genesis 1:2, something happened. We are informed that what was created became "formless and empty, darkness was over the surface of the deep" (Genesis 1:2).

The Hebrew word used in verse 1 for *created* is *bara,* literally meaning just that—creating something out of nothing.[1] However, in verse 2, the Hebrew word describing the earth being formless, empty and covered in darkness is *haya*, which means to become, to happen, to occur.[2]

What does this tell us? In the beginning what was made good apparently *became* bad. How? Numbers of theologians believe this is when the angel Lucifer fell because of his pride (see Isaiah 14:11–15; Ezekiel 28:13–18).

From the beginning of time, however, we see the marvelous, compassionate way that God responds to catastrophes. After realizing that what He created was now covered with darkness, God didn't decide to just abandon it. No. He refashioned this planet that had lost its original beauty.

When this was done, "God saw all that he had made, and it was *very good*" (Genesis 1:31, emphasis mine). Now if God who is perfect thinks something is very good, it *is* very good. In fact, His new earth became the home for His Son's bride. It was definitely not a second-best place.

Not long after the introduction of the first man and woman, another great failure occurred. These human beings formed from the clay of the earth by God's own hands, made in His own image, fell prey to the deceiver, and Paradise was lost.

An angel with a flaming sword was posted at the entrance to the Garden of Eden so they would never be able to return (see Genesis 3:24). What was God going to do now after the whole purpose of man's creation—fellowship with Him—was lost? Well, He immediately gave them a most wonderful prophecy, the promise of the seed of the woman, who is the Lord Jesus Christ, our Savior (see Genesis 3:15).

Does this mean the cross was God's second best because His first plan for mankind failed when Adam fell? If we say that the coming of the Messiah and the cross (and what Jesus accomplished through His death) were an inferior choice next to God's original plan, it would be blasphemy!

God's gift, "the Lamb slain from the foundation of the world" (Revelation 13:8, NKJV), was God's greatest revelation of His love toward mankind, greater than what Adam ever experienced before his fall. And think about this: The original plan only made man in the image of God, whereas the second one made him a child of God (John 1:12). No, the cross is not second best—it is the very best![3]

After the Fall

From this point onward, man fails. Yet through this, we can still see how God magnificently weaves together His amazing plan from the beginning of history.

Abraham. Further into the book of Genesis, we encounter Abraham. He had faith not only to leave his homeland and set out on a God-given quest, but also the faith to receive a child in his old age. And not just any child— this was the child of promise, the embryo of a great nation that would eventually number more than the sands of the seashore.

Along the way, however, this faith hero fell into lies and deception. Because he was afraid for his life, Abraham told his attractive wife to inform the Egyptian pharaoh that she was his sister rather than his wife (see Genesis 12:10–20).

Not only that, after Abraham received the promise from God that he would have innumerable descendants, impatience got the best of him. Thinking God could produce the son without Sarah, he had a sexual relationship with her servant who conceived a child (see Genesis 16:1–2).

After all this, God restored him, used him mightily and even brought His own Son Jesus into the world through Abraham's line. As a matter of fact, the whole Christian world of those who believe are children of Abraham (see Galatians 3:6–9).

Samson. This powerhouse of a man was called by God to deliver Israel from the hands of the Philistines (see Judges 13:5). Yet he lacked moral conviction and common sense when it came to women. There came a day when it looked like Samson's folly totally destroyed what God wanted to do through him. Samson was forced to serve the very enemies he was born to conquer.

Yet once again, the Lord made the reworked vessel better than the former one. Scripture reports that Samson did more to deliver Israel from the hands of the Philistines after his failure than he did in his 20 years of leading Israel (see Judges 16:30). Resaid, God was still able to bring about His perfect plan through Samson's life.

Thomas. Everyone thinks of him as "doubting Thomas." This privileged man walked with Jesus during His ministry on earth and knew Him face-to-face.

Unfortunately, when the other disciples had the opportunity to see their Lord after He was raised from the dead, Thomas did not. Their excited reports seemed too good for him to believe. "Whoa," responded the absentee. "Unless I see the nail marks in his hands and put my finger where the nails were, and put my hand into his side, I will not believe it" (John 20:25). Before long, the day came when he stood face-to-face with his Lord, and in the presence of his colleagues, he came to grips with his lack of faith.

I'm sure Thomas was grieved by his own skepticism, this reluctance to believe that Jesus could do something so amazing. But was that the end of his usefulness to the Lord?

No. Again, the Potter made a more beautiful vessel than what was there before. He chose Thomas to go to one of the hardest regions in the world at that time, to far-off India. Through his great faith and ultimate martyrdom, this extraordinary disciple established the Church in my nation.

In fact, in A.D. 52 Thomas traveled to Niranam (the village where I was born), shared the Gospel and established a church. And 1,900 years later, God granted me the privilege of being born into a family of believers in that very village. So my spiritual life traces its roots to the labor of Thomas so many generations back. I personally am convinced God was able to bring about His perfect will in the life of this one who earlier was a doubter.

Mark. This is the young man who deserted his teammates on his first missionary assignment. In the Apostle Paul's opinion, Mark was unfit for service and didn't deserve a second chance (see Acts 15:36–38).

How devastated John Mark must have felt about this! But the end of his story had not yet been written. Later on, his presence was desired by the same Apostle Paul, because "he is helpful to me in my ministry" (2 Timothy 4:11).

Mark also became a blessing to the whole Church by writing the story of Jesus in our second Gospel. What an encouragement he was not just in his own lifetime, but to the many ages that have followed.

Time and time again, God has taken marred pots and turned them into vessels of His praise. Not only does He make them more beautiful, but through them, He also brings about His perfect will. Truly, His ways are above our ways.

Sin and Failure—Good or Bad?

So if God is able to bring about His perfect will even though we sin, is there any reason to avoid the traps into which we so easily fall? Why press so hard toward the mark when everything seems to work out well even when we fail?

Pay attention! Although God's grace abounds to us—His ways far above our understanding—and He is able to transform our failure, don't trample under foot the Son of God and treat His blood as an unholy thing by deliberately sinning (see Hebrews 10:26–29).

Paul also addresses this issue in Romans 3:

"But," some say, "our sins serve a good purpose, for people will see God's goodness when he declares us sinners to be innocent. . . . " If you follow that kind of thinking, however, you might as well say that the more we sin the better it is! Those who say such things deserve to be condemned, yet some slander me by saying this is what I preach! (Romans 3:5a, 8, NLT).

Because he often writes about the grace of God for fallen man, Paul reports that some say he is preaching that we should sin more so others will better be able to observe this grace. Nothing could be further from the truth. Later in Romans 6:2 (NLT), he responds to such accusations, saying, "Of course not! Since we have died to sin, how can we continue to live in it?"

Yet the fact remains that no one is righteous. We all fail. But we don't have to continue to live in sin. God's grace is always there to help us become better people. We should be maturing children who bring Him praise—not just for the sake of His grace, but for the work of God to restore that which sin destroys.

But How Can This Be?

Are you still wrestling with, "How can God bring about His perfect will when I messed up so completely? I mean, I deliberately did what God did not want me to do. How can His 'perfect' will still be accomplished in my life?" You are not alone in your struggles.

If we looked at every single Bible illustration in which God did this precise thing, we still would not fully "understand" it. Actually, it is not possible to totally grasp this concept with our finite minds. His ways are far above ours. God views our lives from a totally different vantage point. He knows the end and how He intends to get us there.

First of all, He is not working within the confines of time. C.S. Lewis explains, "Every . . . moment from the beginning of the world—is always the Present for Him."[4] God is eternal. To God, 1 day is like 1,000 years, and 1,000 years is like 1 day. He sees the moment of a failure in our life at the same time He sees us on that moment when we stand before Him as a faultless bride. He sees us the moment we were born at the same time He sees us at the moment of our last breath. He is not restricted to seeing time progress in chronological order. He is not confined in time as we are.

Not only does He have that amazing perspective, but He also is preparing us for eternity, not for tomorrow, not for next year, not even for our lifetime on earth. We so easily evaluate if we are on course by our current achievements, the opinions of men and *our* own view of what we are aiming toward, and our current status. But we forget, we are made *not* for time, but for eternity. All that happens in our lives is a classroom in which God is preparing us to reign with Him throughout eternity.

Can you believe God has something much greater in mind than simply your reputation among the people you are with this very day?

He has thoughts about us that go far beyond what we can even begin to consider. He is working outside of our realm of reference. None of us can totally understand God and His ways with our limited minds. We simply aren't capable.

But we can believe Him. We don't have to understand everything to accept what He says is true. If God says it, we must believe it.

Don't fall into the trap in which you will only believe God if you completely understand Him. Your unbelief will hinder the transformation He wants to bring about in your life. Please don't be a doubter. Join your heart with His and simply believe.

Choose to let go of *yesterday* and embrace the gift of all the *todays* that the Lord Himself has lavished upon you.

CHAPTER FIVE

Take Heart

In the 1950s, Charles Templeton was a household name among evangelical Christians. He was a close friend of Dr. Billy Graham and the pastor of a large and growing church in Toronto, Canada. He was also a mighty evangelist and in some ways was more eloquent and able than Dr. Graham. Many predicted that Charles would become one of the most famous preachers in history. Together, Graham and Templeton had founded Youth for Christ in Canada.

Not that many years later, news came out that Charles Templeton had walked away from the truth of the Scriptures and the God he had proclaimed to millions. Templeton declared himself to now be an agnostic, and his announcement sent shockwaves through the church world.

In spite of his disbelief in a loving God, Templeton continued to give much thought to God and his struggles with Christianity over the rest of his life. He wrote several books about these concepts with which he grappled. In 1999, Templeton published his last book, titled *Farewell to God.* The book's subtitle was *My Reasons for Rejecting the Christian Faith.*

Author Lee Strobel was fascinated with the volume and sought an interview with the Canadian to gain more understanding into this man's journey. Strobel ended up writing his book *The Case for Faith* in response to that meeting. In it, Strobel recounts that eventful conversation.

Strobel had gone to Templeton's high-rise apartment in Toronto to sit with this 83-year-old man. At the time, Templeton's health was failing with Alzheimer's. For some minutes, Strobel pressed Templeton about his beliefs in God. Growing more strong and adamant, Templeton made it clear that he could not reconcile believing in a God who seemed to permit random cruelty and evil. He stood his intellectual ground, giving no hint that anything could change his hardened position.

Strobel then turned the interview toward Jesus. An article from *Christian Courier* comments on their conversation as follows:

How would he now assess Jesus at this stage of his life?

Strobel says that, amazingly, Templeton's "body language softened." His voice took on a "melancholy and reflective tone." And then, incredibly, he said:

"He was the greatest human being who has ever lived. He was a moral genius. His ethical sense was unique. He was the intrinsically wisest person that I've ever encountered in my life or in my reading. His commitment was total and led to his own death, much to the detriment of the world."

. . . Strobel quietly commented: "You sound like you really care about him."

"Well, yes," Templeton acknowledged, "he's the most important thing in my life." He stammered: "I . . . I . . . I adore him. . . . Everything good I know, everything decent I know, everything pure I know, I learned from Jesus."

Strobel was stunned. He listened in shock. He says that Templeton's voice began to crack. He then said, "I . . . miss . . . him!" With that the old man burst into tears; with shaking frame, he wept bitterly.[1]

Somehow, this minister who early in life was a strong Christian leader lost his faith. He let go of the Jesus he loved so dearly. How could something like that happen?

C.S. Lewis writes in his book *Mere Christianity*, "We must never imagine that our own unaided efforts can be relied on to carry us through the next twenty-four hours as 'decent' people. If He does not support us, not one of us is safe from some gross sin."[2]

No one is immune to failure.

No matter how much knowledge or experience or revelation one might have, no one is exempt from tripping spiritually. None of us should ever presume to have "arrived" or to be stable enough not to fall, even significantly. Not even a spiritual stalwart who has been faithful for the past 50 years is immune to crashing.

The Bible warns us in 1 Corinthians 10:12, "If you think you are standing firm, be careful that you don't fall!" I pray that in the areas in which you believe yourself to be strong that you choose to humble yourself. Be careful to continue in His grace, for He gives grace to the *humble*, but by His own Word, He must oppose the proud (see James 4:6).

May Your Faith Not Fail

Jesus sat eating the Last Supper with His disciples, sharing His final words with them hours before He was to be seized, brought to trial and crucified. In this setting, He turned to Peter and said, "Simon, Simon, Satan has asked to sift you as wheat. But I have prayed for you, Simon, that your faith may not fail.

And when you have turned back, strengthen your brothers" (Luke 22:31–32).

Jesus knew Peter was going to deny Him. I find it interesting that His prayer was *not* that Peter wouldn't fail. Jesus did not seem as concerned about Peter failing as He was that his *faith* would not fail.

Why was our Lord more concerned about Peter's faith than his failure?

Our faith in God and in His goodness is the safety rope that pulls us out of whatever pit in which we find ourselves. If we believe God and believe He is good, no matter where we are, that safety rope will get us out. Even when contrary to the feelings of the moment, simply affirming with conviction, "I believe You, God. I believe that You are good," will get us on the road again.

But if we stop believing in God and His goodness, we are without a safety rope and have no way to climb out of our pit.

Charles Templeton had lost that critical safety rope—his belief in God and His goodness. Without it, he could not get back on the road to recovery. I believe that just as with Peter, Jesus is not necessarily praying to the Father that you will not fail, but that in the midst of it your faith will not fail. God doesn't want you to forget His faithfulness.

Although God will *not* prevent you from

failure, He will ensure that Satan won't test you to the point of ruin, just as He did with Peter. You see, today Jesus is interceding for you (see Romans 8:34).

All of us must remember this truth that even when we are unfaithful, He remains faithful (see 2 Timothy 2:13). God's goodness and love toward us will never change. "Put your hope in the LORD, for with the LORD is unfailing love and with him is full redemption" (Psalm 130:7).

So even when all seems dark and hopeless, I too pray that your faith will not falter. Even when all emotions and feelings dry up, hang on by faith, knowing that His love toward you is constant, as sure as the rising sun.

Is There a Purpose?

If no one is *immune* to failure and if God will not *prevent* failure, could it be that God has a *purpose* in it?

I believe so.

God's purpose in our failure is that we become more like His Son, Jesus. Jesus described Himself only once in Scripture. He said, "I am gentle and humble in heart" (Matthew 11:29). It is the pride within our hearts that is most contrary to Christ and the most like Satan. Yet pride is the sin that so easily runs rampant in the human heart.

Failure is one of God's best tools to transform our prideful hearts into a heart like His. God allowed Peter to fail and be sifted. As a result, he was cleansed of so much chaff in his life. He was made more like Christ than he had ever been before.

God will allow Satan to sift us too. There is chaff in all of us—the chaff of pride, self-confidence and self-righteousness. If we let Him, He can fashion in us a soft heart of gentleness and humility. Jesus prompts us, "Come . . . and learn from me, for I am gentle and humble in heart, and you will find rest for your souls. For my yoke is easy and my burden is light" (Matthew 11:28–30).

His invitation is before us. His way is clear. Restoration is near. God wants to bring about His purpose through our failure, but before He can do that, we must come to Jesus and be willing to learn from Him.

What Does He Want to Teach Us?

He wants to teach us to *lean upon God's grace*. Perhaps in the way you failed, you will finally be able to realize that you cannot make it on your own. Temptation and failures are like the law in the Old Testament: They show us our incredible need for grace. C.S. Lewis writes,

> Only those who try to resist temptation
> know how strong it is. After all, you find
> out the strength of the German army by
> fighting against it, not by giving in. . . .
> If there was any idea that God had set us
> a sort of exam, and we might get good
> marks by deserving them, that has been
> wiped out. . . . God has been waiting for
> the moment at which you discover that
> there is no question of earning a pass
> mark in this exam or putting Him in your
> debt.[3]

"For it is by grace you have been saved, through faith—and this not from yourselves, it is the gift of God—not by works, so that no one can boast" (Ephesians 2:8–9). It is through our failures that God often helps us see our need for salvation—both eternal salvation and the daily walking away from the desires of the flesh to pursue those of the Spirit.

Paul asks the question in Romans 7:24, "What a wretched man I am! Who will rescue me from this body of death?" And he answers himself in verse 25: "Thanks be to God— through Jesus Christ our Lord!" So finally we realize we cannot walk down this road and not fail, except through Jesus Christ our Lord.

Through this revelation of God's grace in our lives and our critical need for the Lord, *humility naturally unfolds in our hearts,* affecting the way we view ourselves, the way we view God and the way we view others. It chips away at our strong exteriors and prideful hearts, helping us realize that if it weren't for the Lord's mercy and grace, we would all be consumed.

It is with this new understanding that God can bring about *true victory* in our lives. Bible teacher and friend Zac Poonen says, "Genuine victory over sin is always accompanied by the deepest humility."[4] God wants us to have that victory. He has promised us that He will never allow us to be tempted beyond what we are able to bear (see 1 Corinthians 10:13).

Yet so often it seems that victory eludes us. It is when our self-confidence is finally destroyed and is replaced with dependence upon God that we have victory.

Jesus encouraged His disciples just before His arrest to "pray so that you will not fall into temptation" (Luke 22:46). He knew that only with dependence on the Lord would they be able to stand. "Unless the LORD builds the house, its builders labor in vain" (Psalm 127:1).

God transforms not only our relationship with Him, but also our relationships with others. God begins to do *a work of compassion* in our hearts. Our failure helps us see that we are no different from any other human being. We are as prone to failure as anyone else. A heart of hard judgment turns into a heart of compassion when we identify in a real and practical way with the rest of flawed humanity.

Several years ago, a pastor and friend of mine was in a terrible car accident. He fell asleep at the wheel, hit a post at high speed and crashed the car. His wife died instantly, and he was in the hospital with complications of all kinds.

Not long after the accident, I visited him in the hospital. It was difficult to see a man of God not just suffering physically, but also bearing the emotional strain of having lost his wife in such a tragic way.

As I spoke with him beside his hospital bed, he said, "I buried so many people and comforted so many in their loss and pain. But for the first time in my life, I understand the meaning of sorrow and death. I feel now the way death separates and removes the people who are most dear, leaving a gaping emptiness within. The one I love is gone. She will never come back on this earth."

As he started to cry, he said, "Now when I go to comfort others, the words I speak will be different than before. I have been in their shoes. I have experienced their pain."

Jesus told Peter, "And when you have turned back, strengthen your brothers." It is only when we are broken that we have the right kind of strength to strengthen others.

It was only when Peter was weak and broken that he became truly strong—so much so that he was able to strengthen his brothers and sisters. We could say that Peter's preparation for that Spirit-filled service on Pentecost came through his experience of failure. Without his encounter with his own shortcomings, he would have stood up to preach on that day as an arrogant man—one who had not failed and who would look down with ridicule at the poor, lost sinners in front of him.

God would have become his enemy, for God resists the proud. Peter had to come to such an incredible low before he could be what God intended. Peter himself realized this truth and warned other Christians, in essence saying, "Don't forget how you yourself were once cleansed from your sins" (see 2 Peter 1:9). He goes on to caution them that if they forget, they will become blind and shortsighted.[5]

This principle is also true for us. God uses temptations and failures to remove the chaff from our lives. He is breaking us so that like a branded animal, we too can bend our necks from our pride and put on Christ's yoke. He is molding us into the image of His own Son: *He is making us holy.*

Therefore, when we fail, let us trust God's sanctifying work in us and look to Him to fulfill His purposes, for He who has called us is faithful (see 1 Corinthians 1:9).

Whether the Lord is succeeding in fulfilling this end in your life or not, you alone know. But if the chaff is being removed, you will be humbler and less self-righteous. You won't look down on others who fail. You won't consider yourself better than anyone else. You will become more like Jesus.

Let us learn from *Him*.

CHAPTER SIX

After Failure

Years ago a man came to me seeking counsel. He served as a full-time minister and was very well-known for his extraordinary giftings. Within the first few minutes of our time together, he broke down weeping. I could hardly make out what he was saying because of his intense sobbing. Finally, through his tears, he voiced his deep pain with these few words—"I lost it all. I failed." He had fallen into adultery.

His sorrow was deep and his repentance more sincere than any I have ever witnessed. He knew the depths of his failure and was crying out for mercy and hope, wanting to believe they were still available to him. By the grace of God, I was able to speak the words he needed to hear and to pray with him.

Years later I learned that this gentleman who took such a hard fall had fully recovered. God's grace was lavished upon him and brought restoration. Now his life and his gifts were being used in multiplied ways, more than he ever thought possible after such a moral failure. Through the years, I have witnessed similar situations, revealing the gracious way God works.

There is an irony here, however. I have also witnessed younger brothers, placed in less influential settings, fall in minor ways and lose it all. There is no adultery or murder, yet these who failed in what many would consider smaller ways are sometimes driven out of the ministry by what they have done.

It makes me wonder, "What happened?" The veteran who should have been wiped out from the ministry is restored and thrives, his life being used to touch thousands of people, while the rookie who really didn't steal all that much lost out completely. How do you explain this?

It's not the size of our sin that determines whether or not we recover from a fall. It's our response. How we deal with our failure determines our future.

God desires to make your life into something beautiful and bring about His purposes through your failure. He wants to accomplish

56

His *perfect* will in your life, but He is waiting on you.

Just as there are real-life examples from Scripture and the people we know who demonstrate God's great skill to still bring about His best in the midst of failure, there are also real-life examples of those who never fully recover. So there is still a question of whether God's best for your life will be experienced. It is yet to be decided . . . by you!

How will you handle what is before you? Will you surrender your heart and your ways to the Lord and let Him do His work of humility within you? Or will your pride rise up and keep you captive to a life that never fully recovers?

Today He is rooting for you. I also encourage you with all my heart to take these simple steps to recovery and a life that refuses to settle for second best.

It Begins with Honesty

God tells us that He desires honesty in our inward parts (see Psalm 51:6, NLT). Honesty is the foundation of all good things God does in and through us.

In Ephesians 6, *truth* is the first piece of spiritual armor we are told to put on. This belt of truth is worn around our waist, the middle of our bodies and the center of our balance.

Honesty and truth must be in place before anything else because they keep us from losing our balance and falling.

This is not the truth that is simply the opposite of lying. Instead, it is a willingness to come before the Lord without any excuses and sit quietly, letting Him search out our heart. It is an openness to hearing His still small voice that all too often people keep trying to cover up. Then we must listen closely for what He says.

Only then will you be able to understand, without justification and explanation, without twisting the truth to put yourself in a more favorable light, the gravity of what you have done. It may be painful for the moment, but this truth will set you free. The Lord can then begin His cleansing in your heart. This cleansing by His Spirit far outweighs any brief moments of pain.

C.S. Lewis explains it further, "It is impossible for Him to show Himself to a man whose whole mind and character are in the wrong condition. Just as sunlight . . . cannot be reflected in a dusty mirror as clearly as a clean one."[1]

It is in this experience of exposure, this act of truly being transparent before the Lord, that the way is cleared for the Spirit to really work in your life. It is the beginning of a deeper work and the foundation for accomplishing His *perfect will* for your life.

Out of this honesty with the Lord, you can truly admit you have failed and ask for His forgiveness. This is the first step to restored intimacy with God and others. C.S. Lewis states, "A man who admits no guilt can accept no forgiveness."[2]

For each one to whom God's best was restored, the road to recovery began with honesty and admitting their failure: from David who told Nathan, "I have sinned against the LORD" (2 Samuel 12:13), to Jacob who finally admitted both his name and his character was Jacob, the deceiver (Genesis 32:27), to the thief on the cross who affirmed that he deserved his judgment (Luke 23:41).

It was in those moments of truth for each of these men that their restoration began: that Nathan told David the Lord took away his sin and he was not going to die (2 Samuel 12:13), that Jacob's name was changed to Israel, the prince of God (Genesis 32:28), that Jesus informed the thief on the cross that today he would be with Him in paradise (Luke 23:43).

In those moments of honesty, the Lord may also show you practical steps of restoration that He wants you to take. Listen to His voice and act on what He puts on your heart. The present awkwardness is nothing in contrast to the joy of our inner man being clear before God and man.

Be aware that admitting your failure in honesty before the Lord is the exact opposite of what your flesh wants to do. When Adam and Eve sinned, their first reaction was to run for cover. Shame entered the scene, and ever since, humanity has tried to hide its failure.

The reason? Simply pride, the desire to keep who we are intact.

I advise you against this. You will only put up a roadblock on your way to recovery. You cannot skip this part and move on to the next step. It begins here or ends here.

Some hide not only from the searching of God's light, but also from those who know their failure. Though sorrowful over the way they failed, their pride keeps them captive. They go through life cutting off relationships and avoiding those who know their flaws, never admitting any wrong and never fully recovering.

Don't let the fear of man hinder what God has in store for you. Go ahead—meet that person, make that call, send that email. Return what you owe. Ask for forgiveness. For the "fear of man will prove to be a snare" (Proverbs 29:25). The brief pain of reality doesn't compare to the lasting joy and peace experienced in God's restoration.

Step into the cleansing and the new life that awaits you.

Accept God's Forgiveness

You must next accept God's forgiveness. Many people today say God forgave them, but they still live with their failures clouding their lives and casting shadows over their days. They really have not *believed* His forgiveness.

When others have not forgiven us, it can be difficult to cling to the Lord's forgiveness. We almost feel it is wrong to accept God's forgiveness when others are still hurting.

Yet it is not wrong. It is God's desire that we accept His gift of forgiveness and journey on the road to restoration. Give others the time and space that they need to work through their struggles. But we must receive with gladness the gift God has given us.

The Lord makes it clear in His Word: "If we confess our sins, he is faithful and just and will forgive us our sins and purify us from all unrighteousness" (1 John 1:9). What He has told us, we must simply believe.

You see, it is God's free gift of righteousness. Notice I said *free*—it is not something we earn. Sanctification, yes—we fail, repent, grow continually day-by-day, becoming more like Jesus. But righteousness is not a growing process; it is simply a gift from God.

We are made righteous in Jesus, through the Father's grace. It says in Romans, "God will credit righteousness—for us who believe in him who raised Jesus our Lord from the dead. He was delivered over to death for our sins and was raised to life for our justification" (Romans 4:24–25). When Jesus died on the cross, provision for sin was made. We can be washed clean. Before God, it is as though our sin never happened.

Can you imagine—the divorce never occurred or the cheating never took place? You never lied or lusted. You never fought with anyone. You never thought evil. You never committed murder. Through Christ, you are made as pure as the day God made Adam and Eve. This is difficult for our minds to grasp and our hearts to believe—but it's true. When God looks at you, He now sees the righteousness of Jesus.

Receive His forgiveness that washes you white as snow.

Resist the Enemy

Our enemy prowls around "like a roaring lion looking for someone to devour" (1 Peter 5:8). In vulnerable times when we are face-to-face with failure, Satan seeks to discourage us to the point where we lose all hope.

At such times, we can become so introspective that we wallow in despair and forget the grace and forgiveness God has given us. We become so preoccupied with our failures that our enemy wins the battle against us simply because we give up.

If we are to stand against this roaring lion, we must realize that a defeated mind-set is not from God; then we must—absolutely must—resist the devil and his lies.

Our faith, the blood of Jesus and our testimony are powerful weapons to resist the enemy who seeks to destroy all hope for the future and the plans God has for us.

Ephesians 6:16 tells us that we must take up our shield of faith by which we can quench the enemy's fiery darts and stand against this accuser of the brethren. By the sacrifice and blood of Jesus, Satan's head was crushed. By our testimony, we confess with our mouth Jesus' victory over the enemy. We refuse to accept thoughts of confusion, accusation, guilt, condemnation and whatever else he may conjure up. We reject these because of what Jesus did for us and because we are "accepted in the beloved" (Ephesians 1:6, KJV).

Then what happens? "The accuser of our brothers, who accuses them before our God day and night, *has been hurled down*. They overcame him by the blood of the Lamb and by the word of their testimony" (Revelation 12:10–11, emphasis mine).

The devil is a defeated foe. Don't be fooled by his blustering.

Believe God

In every step of this process, we must believe God. It says in Hebrews 11:6, "And without faith it is impossible to please God, because anyone who comes to him must believe that he exists and that he rewards those who earnestly seek him."

Along this journey of restoration, every step requires that we believe His Word regardless of our feelings.

So—we must believe there is hope. We must believe that His best remains. We must believe that His road of humility is better than our road of pride. We must believe His restoration is more important than our reputation. We must believe He truly forgives us. And we must believe that by His blood, Satan's head was crushed.

The answer for which you are searching lies in believing God. This is a life of faith. Our salvation started with it, and our journey on earth will end with our first act of faith becoming sight. And all along the journey, the only way we continue strong is by faith—faith in God and in His goodness.

He is constantly working with us and is able to finish the good work that He started (see Philippians 1:6).

My brothers and sisters, nothing, *absolutely nothing,* is impossible with our God.

CHAPTER SEVEN

On the Other Side

He was a lawyer—a good one. He demanded the best of himself, and nothing less was acceptable.

But he didn't stop there. He also required the best from everyone else. Unfortunately, few could meet his standards. The truth is, there was little joy in being around him, because tension seemed to shadow him.

Then a day came when everything changed. In the wrong place at the wrong time, he was accidentally shot. He lived, but lost many of the simple skills most people take for granted. He had to relearn how to tie his shoes and even how to talk. As he was forced to practice basic tasks over and over again, his personality began to change.

One day while sitting at the breakfast table, his young daughter accidentally spilled her orange juice. She looked up fearfully at her father. Before, he never would have tolerated such clumsiness.

This time, however, he looked kindly at her and asked, "What's wrong?" Instead of being upset, he purposely knocked over his own orange juice and said, "It's okay. Look. I do it all the time." Then the father and his daughter laughed together.

What a story. What a change in this man's makeup. But what happened?

When his own performance standards were so high, he had little patience for others. But constantly faced with his own mistakes, he afforded others the same grace he so badly needed.

Of the Same Cloth

Whether or not we realize it, we all have our own set of standards by which we tend to measure others. How many times do we shake our heads at people and think, "What is wrong with this guy anyway? Why is she struggling with that? Why don't they just . . ." In our heads, we impose a perfection that they aren't measuring up to. We can be especially critical about matters with which we don't struggle, the areas of our own strength.

We behave like the man in Scripture who was forgiven a great sum yet was unwilling to show mercy to a fellow servant who by comparison owed only a few pennies (see Matthew 18:23–34).

God forbid that we would have to get shot in order to learn how to be gracious. Who rejoices over a cure that's worse than the disease?

But how do we get to the place at which we initially respond to others out of compassion? This is an issue with which I myself have a great struggle. Do you ever find yourself complaining about a co-worker for an extended period of time? Do you rake family members over the coals for the obvious ways they are failing? How often do you catch yourself in these patterns before you even realize what you're doing?

Jesus said, "If any one of you is without sin, let him be the first to throw a stone at her" (John 8:7).

You know this story: A young lady was dragged before Jesus by the religious crowd. She had failed big time. She was caught in adultery, and now by law she must be stoned to death. Jesus was challenged to give His judgment. The tension was thick.

Christ answered, "If any one of you is without sin, let him be the first to throw a stone." What do you think He was saying to that smug group of people?

Did He say, "He who has not committed adultery like this woman can cast the first stone"?

No. He said, "If any one of you is *without* sin . . ." (emphasis mine). If none of us can say we are without sin, then Jesus must want us to take a different approach. How does this sound? "I understand that you struggle. Guess what? I struggle too. But we will get there. We will get there together. So let's help one another."

Even the greatest saints and the most successful workers in God's kingdom have experienced discouragement and failure in their lives. Charles Spurgeon one time confessed, "I am the subject of depression of spirit so fearful that I hope none of you ever gets to such extreme of wretchedness as I go through."

Believe it or not, we are all pretty much cut from the same piece of cloth. Some of us are clever and are able to hide our problems, but we are still much the same on the inside. And within that realization lies our answer.

Christ who knew no sin showed compassion to this woman, saying, "Neither do I condemn you" (John 8:11). How much more should we, who know all too well the sting of sin and failure, show compassion to our brothers and sisters?

God expects this of us. He assumes we will use the experience of our failures and His restoration to aid in helping others who have fallen. It only makes sense. In 2 Corinthians 1:4 (NASB) Paul says, "[God] comforts us in all our affliction so that we will be able to comfort those who are in any affliction with the comfort with which we ourselves are comforted by God."

You Be My Jesus

Sometime back, a friend shared with me some of his burdens. I listened prayerfully, asking the Lord to help me understand what he was going through.

One after another he talked about discouragements and failures that seemed to have gotten the best of him. He said he still read his Bible and prayed, but it all seemed so lifeless; what he felt was that God Himself had forsaken him.

His wish was that he could quit everything and just run away. "I am in a fast-moving train, and I am so tired. I just want to get off, but this train isn't stopping for me." Tears fell unchecked. His whole body seemed to bend under a staggering load.

I sensed the Lord asking me if I would represent the compassionate, caring, restoring person of Jesus in my words to this man.

Thank God the story ends well. After listening for a long time, I shared my heart and laid my hands on him and prayed. He left the room a changed individual. This prayer on behalf of the Lord brought recovery, and a month later he was serving the Lord with the excitement and energy he had before.

Right after he left my room, the words, "You be my Jesus," came to my mind. I realized how we all need that physical touch of someone who will be the ministry of Jesus to us.

The following is the poem I wrote from that encounter:

The night is darker than the darkest night
not a star in the sky.
Cruel storm howls in distance
creating piercing silence.
Nonstop downpour.
It seems this night is forever.

My lamp is empty
only left the smoking wick
hurting my eyes
forcing me to shut them in the dark.

Is there anyone who cares
to understand
to say a kind word
to lend a helping hand?

Yes, I know Jesus cares
Jesus understands.

But I don't see Him
　　　can't touch Him
　　　　　Where is He?

Till I find Him
Please stay with me
Please take my hand.

It is so dark.
YOU BE MY JESUS
I am all alone.
　　　Alone.[1]

The Lord wants us to take on this ministry to others during such dark times—to be His ears, to be His hands, to be His mouth, to represent Him. Maybe you will meet someone today who, without words, is saying to you, "You be my Jesus."

The Picture of Compassion

Some years ago, when I described to my wife my frustration about a given individual— a very difficult person to deal with—she said to me, "You are forgetting something: God wants him to succeed. We must cooperate with God and work toward that end." The Lord used her words to change my thinking.

Jesus is a picture we can look at of what God our Father is like (see John 14:9). Through His example, we can learn how to be the "ministry of Jesus" to others. This way we can cooperate with what God our Father wants to do in our world.

One example from Jesus' life is the encounter He had with the Samaritan woman (see John 4:5–42). She had been the object of town gossip, and to even be remotely associated with her was a public disgrace.

I am sure she spent her days trying to ignore her various "judges" around the village as well as her inner struggle with the sin in which she kept finding herself—five failed marriages and now she was living with a man.

But Jesus, a Jew, talked graciously to her. (It was not appropriate for Jews to speak to Samaritans because they were considered the low caste.) Our Lord, however, did not talk down to her. He didn't make her feel small like everyone else probably did.

Yes, He brought up the matter of her sin. But in spite of this, she didn't defend herself or leave. Apparently she felt welcome in His presence. If she sensed in Him any disdain toward her, even if she had "discerned" Him a prophet by His word of knowledge, I don't believe she would have lingered for very long.

Jesus did not preach a three-point sermon about the wrong turns she had made in life and what she needed to do differently. Instead, He welcomed her into the kingdom—transforming and restoring her by His love.

When He sensed her need, His response was an overwhelming tide of compassion. So much so that He wasn't even hungry anymore.

Later we see Jesus at the pool of Bethesda (John 5:1–15). Here He learned there was a man who had been ill for a long time. Upon hearing this news, Jesus reached out and healed him instantly.

Because of sin, this man had been sick for 38 years. Yet the Lord granted him a new beginning and a new life. Our Lord could very well have exposed his sin to those who stood around and made it into a great sermon illustration.

Only later, when Jesus was alone with him, did He tell him, "Stop sinning or something worse may happen" (John 5:14).

Through these examples, we see Christ's respect for the dignity of others, His unconditional forgiveness and His loving honesty. Galatians 6:1 (NKJV) says, ". . . restore such a one in a spirit of gentleness."

Paul says in Philippians 2:5 (NKJV), "Let this mind be in you which was also in Christ Jesus." So we are called to be partakers of the nature of our Lord Jesus Christ. These are the same characteristics God wants us to use as we minister to those who have failed. Again, we are challenged to walk in the footsteps of Jesus. He is our example.

No matter where we go, we are surrounded by people who have failed and are still hurting. Most of them are desperately lonely. Let us extend Christ's compassion to them. What these people need is the Lord.

Together, let us learn to say, "I struggle too. But we can get there together."

Conclusion

I t is a new day.
 The morning light is shining through the window. Before you is a clean slate, never written on before. There *is* hope.

Yesterday has passed. The gift of today has been granted to you. Walk in it. Walk by His light. Walk in dependence on Him.

Remember His great grace and the height of your fall. Never forget it was His restoration and not your own work.

Embrace the promise that His perfect plan for your life is still before you. The best is yet to come.

Overcomers are not those who have never failed, but those who overcame by the blood that was shed for their sins. Christ's blood is only useful for people willing to admit they have failed and in this confession find the way of victory.

Whenever you wonder, "What next?" remember that your Father in heaven still loves you. Receive His gracious forgiveness and embrace it as another opportunity to be humbled and Christlike.

Even now, if necessary, get up and go home. Your Father is waiting for you.

If this booklet has been a blessing to you, I would really like to hear from you. You may write to

Gospel for Asia
1800 Golden Trail Court
Carrollton, TX 75010

Or send an email to kp@gfa.org.

a division of Gospel for Asia

www.gfa.org

Notes

Chapter 1

[1] Robert Robinson, "Come, Thou Fount of Every Blessing" (1758). Public Domain.

[2] *Ibid.*

[3] K.P. Yohannan, "There Is Hope."

[4] Robinson, "Come, Thou Fount of Every Blessing."

Chapter 2

[1] Dale Carnegie, *How to Win Friends and Influence People* (New York, NY: Pocket Books, 1981), pp. 3–4.

[2] Roy Hession, *"When I Saw Him . . ." Where Revival Begins* (Fort Washington, PA: Christian Literature Crusade, 1975), p. 63.

Chapter 3

[1] "When God Wants to Drill a Man," quoted in V. Raymond Edman, *The Disciplines of Life* (Minneapolis, MN: World Wide Publications, 1948), p. 54.

Chapter 4

[1] James Strong, LL.D., S.T.D., *The Strongest Strongs: Exhaustive Concordance of the Bible* (Grand Rapids, MI: Zondervan Publishing, 2001), p. 1371.

[2] *Ibid.*, p. 1380.

[3] Ideas taken from a message shared by Zac Poonen at the Gospel for Asia Biblical Seminary in 1997.

[4] C.S. Lewis, *Mere Christianity* (New York, NY: HarperCollins Publishers, Inc., 1980), p. 167.

Chapter 5

[1] Wayne Jackson, "A Skeptic Reflects upon Jesus Christ" *Christian Courier* (http://www.christiancourier.com/penpoints/skepticReflects.htm).

[2] Lewis, *Mere Christianity*, p. 204.

[3] *Ibid.*, pp. 142–143.

[4] Zac Poonen, *The Purpose of Failure* (Bangalore, India: Christian Fellowship Centre, 2000), p. 29.

[5] Ideas taken from a message shared by Zac Poonen at the Gospel for Asia Biblical Seminary.

Chapter 6

[1] Lewis, *Mere Christianity*, p. 164.

[2] C.S. Lewis, *The Problem of Pain* (New York, NY: Macmillan, 1962), p. 122.

Chapter 7

[1] K.P. Yohannan, "You Be My Jesus."

OTHER BOOKS
BY K.P. YOHANNAN

REVOLUTION IN WORLD MISSIONS

In this exciting and fast-moving narrative, K.P. Yohannan shares how God brought him from his remote jungle village to become the founder of Gospel for Asia.

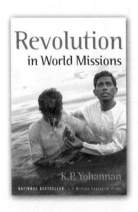

AGAINST THE WIND

In this eye-opening book, K.P. Yohannan challenges you to consider how you are running the race God has set before you. Like the apostle Paul, you too can learn what it takes to be able to one day say, "I have fought the good fight; I have finished the race; I have kept the faith" no matter what the obstacles.

Order online at *www.gfa.org*

THE ROAD TO REALITY

K.P. Yohannan gives an uncompromising call to live a life of simplicity to fulfill the Great Commission.

COME, LET'S REACH THE WORLD

How effective are the Church's current missions strategies? Are the unreached hearing the Gospel? K.P. Yohannan examines the traditional approach to missions—its underlying assumptions, history and fruit—in light of Scripture and the changing world scene. This book is a strong plea for the Body of Christ to partner with indigenous missionaries so that the whole world may hear.

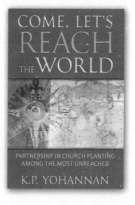

Living in the Light of Eternity

K.P. Yohannan lovingly, yet candidly, reminds Christians of their primary role while here on earth: harvesting souls. This book challenges us to look at our heart attitudes, motivation and our impact on eternity.

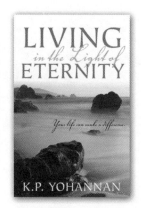

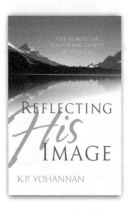

Reflecting His Image

K.P. Yohannan takes us on a journey back to God's original purpose for each of our lives: to reflect His image. This book is a compilation of short, easy-to-read chapters that deal with following Christ closely.

Order online at *www.gfa.org*

JOURNEY WITH JESUS SERIES

A LIFE OF BALANCE

Remember learning how to ride a bike? It was all a matter of balance. The same is true for our lives. Learn how to develop that balance, which will keep your life and ministry healthy and honoring God. (80 pages)

DEPENDENCE UPON THE LORD

Don't build in vain. Learn how to daily depend upon the Lord—whether in the impossible or the possible—and see your life bear lasting fruit. (48 pages)

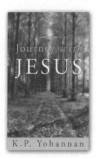

JOURNEY WITH JESUS

Take this invitation to walk the roads of life intimately with the Lord Jesus. Stand with the disciples and learn from Jesus' example of love, humility, power and surrender. (56 pages)

SEEING HIM

Do you often live just day-to-day, going through the routine of life? We so easily lose sight of Him who is our everything. Through this booklet, let the Lord Jesus restore your heart and eyes to see Him again. (48 pages)

STAY ENCOURAGED

How are you doing? Discouragement can sneak in quickly and subtly, through even the smallest things. Learn how to stay encouraged in every season of life, no matter what the circumstances may be. (56 pages)

THAT THEY ALL MAY BE ONE

In this booklet, K.P. Yohannan opens up his heart and shares from past struggles and real-life examples on how to maintain unity with those in our lives. A must read! (56 pages)

Order online at *www.gfa.org*

LEARNING TO PRAY

Whether you realize it or not, your prayers change things. Be hindered no longer as K.P. Yohannan shares how you can grow in your daily prayer life. See for yourself how God still does the impossible through prayer. (64 pages)

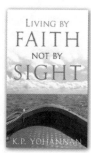

LIVING BY FAITH, NOT BY SIGHT

The promises of God are still true today: *"Anything is possible to him who believes!"* This balanced teaching will remind you of the power of God and encourage you to step out in childlike faith. (56 pages)

PRINCIPLES IN MAINTAINING A GODLY ORGANIZATION

Remember the "good old days" in your ministry? This booklet provides a biblical basis for maintaining that vibrancy and commitment that accompany any new move of God. (48 pages)

THE BEAUTY OF CHRIST THROUGH BROKENNESS

We were made in the image of Christ that we may reflect all that He is to the hurting world around us. Rise above the things that hinder you from doing this, and see how your life can display His beauty, power and love. (72 pages)

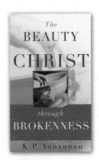

THE LORD'S WORK DONE IN THE LORD'S WAY

Tired? Burned out? Weary? The Lord's work done in His way will never destroy you. Learn what it means to minister unto Him and keep the holy love for Him burning strong even in the midst of intense ministry. A must-read for every believer! (72 pages)

THE WAY OF TRUE BLESSING

What does God value most? Find out in this booklet as K.P. Yohannan reveals truths from the life of Abraham, an ordinary man who became the friend of God. (56 pages)

Order online at *www.gfa.org*